An Anson Primary School publication

All rights reserved

Copyright © 2023 Anson Primary School
Anson Road, London, NW2 4AB

Roundwood
Year One

Sea Animal
Acrostics

PREFACE

In November 2022 the children of Anson Primary School, in North London, had the incredible experience of meeting a dinosaur and a gorilla in the school hall.

The creatures arrived along with the wonderful teach of Teach Rex and inspired the pupils to become more aware of the world around them, the part they play in the care of the planet and how to make their lives more sustainable.

Following the visit each pupil wrote a poetic response to their experience, drawing upon the emotions of the day, the new knowledge and research.

The poems in this book are a snapshot of their thinking. Each poem represents an animal, an emotion or an action for our planet that means something to the children.

In the years to come, when we look back at this book, how these animals will still be thriving? How many rainforests will survive and what changes will we have made to protect our world?

This is Our World, written by the children of Anson.

Michelle Daly
English Leader

Roundwood Year One

Sea Animal Acrostics

PREFACE

In November 2022 the children of Anson Primary School, in North London, had the incredible experience of meeting a dinosaur and a gorilla in the school hall.

The creatures arrived along with the wonderful teach of Teach Rex and inspired the pupils to become more aware of the world around them, the part they play in the care of the planet and how to make their lives more sustainable.

Following the visit each pupil wrote a poetic response to their experience, drawing upon the emotions of the day, the new knowledge and research.

The poems in this book are a snapshot of their thinking. Each poem represents an animal, an emotion or an action for our planet that means something to the children.

In the years to come, when we look back at this book, how these animals will still be thriving? How many rainforests will survive and what changes will we have made to protect our world?

This is Our World, written by the children of Anson.

Michelle Daly
English Leader

Ocean

Octopus dancing in the sea
Crabs clicking all day
Exciting ocean
Angry octopus
New creatures

Emma Fazzini

Sea Life

See fish
Egg laid
Angry fish
Lay eggs
I like crabs
Fish is cure
Egg cracks

Aisha Shahriya

Ocean

Octopus is dancing
Crab can pinch
Egg is laid by the fish
Angry fish
Nice colourful coral

Yhellobelle De Leon

Sea Life

Sea egg
Egg fish
App fish
Lip fish
Ice-cream fish
Fin fish
Egg app fish

Ryan Hani

Ocean

Octopus
Clown fish
Egg
Animals
Net

Aidan Khan

Ocean

Octopus jiggle
Crab pinch me
Eggs lay on floor
Angry fish
Nadia can swim

Nadia Boukrouh

Sea Life

Surrounded clown fish
Eggs, the shark eat
Amazing whales eating
"Look!" the sharks yell
"I'm stuck", said the seahorse
"Fabulous!" said the puffer fish
"Eggs are falling" said sharks

Everest-Yasmeen Buchanan

Sea Life

Sea creatures dancing in the sea
Eggs come from fish
Amazing fish
Look! The shark
I'm like the sea
Fish are funny
Eggs come from sharks

Evelyn Angwin

Ocean

Octopus
Clam
Egg
Amazing
Nice

Ghina Faroukh

Ocean

Octopus
Crab
Egg
Angry
Nice

Aalia Baig

Sea Life

Sharks are scary
Every starfish is cool
Amazing animals
Like the lionfish
Incredible fish
Fish lay eggs
Eggs are lost in the ocean

Martin Torres Sanchez

Sea Animals

Seashell
Egg
Angry fish
Lionfish
Incredible fish
Fish
Egg

Kwasi Kusi

8

Ocean

Octopus in the sea
Clams in the sea
Eggs laid by fish
Angry sharks
Nice fish

Moksh Patel

Sea Life

Some fish are dead
Eggs are cute
Apples
Like fish
In the sea
Frog
Eggs

Sophia Ferreira

Sun

Sun
Up
Nice

Steven Leng
Aishah Ssekagya
Matias Teshome

The Sun

Sunny day
Under the tree
Nice

Lamees Afrouh
Ajwah Mansoor
Elisa Failey
Lorenzo Ferrira Carranza
Emily Boloshi & Suha Saeed

Ocean

Octopus has lumps
Cells are in these
Eels have flickering tails
Angry fish
Nibble said the shark

Markus Yang-Johnson

Ocean

Octopus has three hearts
Clown fish has white stripes
Eel has a swishy tail
Angry fish are scary
Naughty fish are silly

Awsam Nahas

Queen's Year One

Dinosaur Acrostics

No Dinosaurs Are Kind

Dinosaurs eat meat
I like T-rex
No dinosaurs are kind
Oceans
Sharp teeth
A T-rex is tall
Unkind
Roar!

Hadiyah Suleman

Iguanadon

Dinos
Iguanadon
No teeth
Oceans
Scary
Awesome
Up
Roaring

Elena Safari

12

How to Find Dinosaurs

Dinos
Iguanodon
North America
Oceans
Sharp teeth
Africa
Under rocks we hammer
Roar

Julia Fouani

Dinosaurs are coming to London

Dinosaurs are coming to London
I think dinosaurs are scary
No more alive, they don't live
Oh I wonder if anyone has a dinosaur pet
Soon I think dinosaurs will be alive
A dinosaur has big feet
Under the ocean we can find dinosaur feet
Read the dinosaur books

Muhammed Hammid

Dinosaurs

Dinosaurs are orange
Iguanodon is my favourite
Not alive anymore
Omnivores eat meat and plants
Scary dinosaurs like stomping
Attack raptors before they eat you
Unkind dinosaurs fight each other
Raptors move very fast

Shay Bhanderi

Run!

Did you know dinosaurs lived millions of years ago?
I love the T-rex because T-rex is the king.
No more dinosaurs are alive.
Oh dinosaurs are so big.
So run the T-rex is here!
A t-rex is so cool.
Underground you can find fossils.
Rrrr went the T-rex.

Marco Greenidge

14

Sharp Claws and Sharp Teeth

Dinosaurs are carnivores.
I like velociraptor.
Not alive the dinosaurs.
Omnivores eat plants and meat with
Sharp claws and sharp teeth.
A velociraptor has a long tail.
Underground you can find fossils.
Run fast or you will get bitten

Tasneem Jaroudi

Iguanodon

Dangerous
Iguanodon is a
Noisy
Omnivore.
Scary.
Attack!
Usually they have a scary
Roar!

Sviatoslava Turchynets

Sleep Forever

Dinosaurs are scary.
I like the velociraptor.
Now they sleep forever.
Omnivores eat plants and meat with
Sharp claws and sharp teeth.
Angry T-rex likes fighting.
Underground I see fossils.
Run, dinosaur, run!

Jana Konbos

Roar! Roar!

Dinosaurs lived a long time ago and
I really like that dinosaurs don't live anymore.
No! A dinosaur is going to eat me!
Oh no! Dinosaurs are coming!
Stop dinosaur! They are very bad.
A dinosaur is an animal.
Up in the sky pterodactyl's fly.
Roar! Roar! It's a T-rex, run!

Emilia Blin-Zand

16

Dinosaurs are coming!

Dinosaurs are coming!
In the past they were scary but
No more dinosaurs live today.
Oh I just love the velociraptor.
Stegosaurus swings its tail.
All dinosaurs are unique.
Unkind dinosaurs will eat you while
Roaring through the jungle.

Alexander Eaton-White

Dinosaurs

Dinosaurs are kind.
In the past dinosaurs roared.
Never run away.
Omnivores eat meat and plants with
Sharp teeth.
Angry T-rex.
Usually dinos are huge
Running around in dinosaur land.

Kerima Ahmed

Roar!

Dinosaurs are really big
I don't like dinos
No dinosaurs live today
Omnivores eat meat and plants
Sharp teeth
A fossil is found
Unkind
Roar!

Yusra Abdulkadir

Scary Dinosaurs

Dinosaurs are scary.
Iguanodon are there.
No dinosaurs alive.
Oh some dinosaurs are slow.
Scary dinosaurs
And they have sharp claws.
Under the ground are dinosaurs
Roaring and eating meat.

Mahamed Yassin

Unexpected

Deadly dinosaurs
In packs and herds
Never expected an
Object from space to end their days but then,
Suddenly, the meteor
Arrived
Under the
Reddening
Skies.

Mr Pile

What is under the rock?

Dinosaurs have sharp teeth.
I like dinosaur teeth.
No!
Oh no! The dinosaurs are coming!
Scary teeth!
Apatosaurus is so big
Under the rock
Roar!

Ali Khalas, Ahmad Hussain
Aous Al Dahi, Troy Sambo & Eisa Habibi

Dinosaurs

Dinosaurs eat meat.
I like dinosaur eyes.
Not nice! **N**ot nice!
Omnivore!
Sharp teeth!
A T-rex has short arms
Under the rock.
Run!

Ayeza Fraaz

Ikhlas Loves Dinosaurs

Dinosaurs
Ikhlas loves dinosaurs
Noisy
Oceans
Sharp teeth
A sharp tooth
Underground
Roar!

Ikhlas Ahmed Nuur

Dinosaurs

Dinosaurs eat meat and plants.
I really like pterodactyl.
No dinosaurs live anymore.
Oh no! T-Rex ate other dinosaurs.
So what is your favourite dinosaur?
A dinosaur has claws.
Unkind dinosaurs sometimes eat meat.
Rough dinosaurs kill some other dinosaurs.

Mikaela Bonich

Dinosaurs

Dinosaurs are scary.
Iguanodon are tall.
No dinosaurs are alive.
Omnivores eat meat and plants.
Sharp teeth.
A T-Rex has short arms.
Under the rock is a fossil.
Run!

Yusuf Hussain

Regent's
Year Two

Orangutan
Acrostics

Stop!

Orangutans are dying away.
Rally and rumble to save them today.
Animals and people in the rainforest where
Naughty people are cutting down trees.
Going to ruin the forest.
U are hurting them.
They have to stop!
Animals are running away.
Now come on, save them today!

Taima Al Shalabi

Naughty Humans

Orangutans are dying away.
Rally and rumble to save them today.
Animals are feeling bad and we
Need to help them.
Go away naughty humans.
Up the trees we hide.
Trees are not for palm oil.
All of this is a big spoil.
Now come on, **HELP US**!

Sedra Aldahi

Go Orangutans, Go!

Orangutans are dying away.
Rally and rumble to save them today.
Animals, like the orangutan need help,
Now let's save them!
Go Orangutan, go!
Up the trees they hide.
Trees are their home, not for palm oil
Animals are running away!
Now come on, save them today!

Saffiyah Salaria

Orangutans

Orangutans are dying away.
Rally and rumble to save them today.
Animals are dying.
Naughty humans.
Gorillas are dying.
Up the trees they hide,
Trees which are their home.
Animals are running away.
Now come on, save them today!
-

Haitam Ajbar Boulben

Dying

Orangutans are dying away.
Rally and rumble to save them today.
Animals are dead already.
New animals grow in their mum's tummies.
Giant orangutans are dying.
Up the trees they hide.
Trees fall down when people cut them.
Animals are running away!
Now come on, save them today!

Inaaya Rahman

Go Back Home

Orangutans are dying away.
Rally and rumble to save them today.
And the animals are scared.
Now you need to help.
Go back to your home humans.
Up the trees they hide
Till they are cut down.
Animals are running away!
Now come on, save them today!

Minatalah Salah

Save the Orangutans

Orangutans are dying away.
Rally and rumble to save them today.
Animals are running away from their homes
Now stop cutting down the trees!
Go and save the orangutans.
Up the trees they hide
Towering green trees shiver, sway, rattle and shake
Animals are running away!
Now come on, save them today!

Zahra Idress

Stop!

Orangutans are dying away.
Rally and rumble to save them today.
Animal's homes are getting destroyed and
Now trees are getting cut down for palm oil.
Go on save the orangutans.
Up the trees they hide.
Tell the humans to stop!
Animals are running away!
Now come on, save them today!

Seren-Rose Buchanan-Savoury

Naughty

Orangutans are dying away.
Rally and rumble to save them today.
Animals are running away from the rainforest while
Naughty humans are cutting down trees.
Go away naughty humans!
Up in the trees we hide but the
Trees are being chopped down.
Animals are running away!
Now come on, save them today!

Myles Clarke-Waithe

Go is for Go Away!

Orangutans are dying away.
Rally and rumble to save them today.
A day to save them is today so
Nasty people go away!
G is for GO away!
Up the trees they hide but
The orangutans are losing their homes.
Animals are running away!
Now come on, save them today!

Issa Hamade

Orangutans

Orangutans are dying away.
Rally and rumble to save them today.
Animals run away so
Naughty people stop cutting down trees.
Go help now!
U have been bad.
Trees are important and
Animals are running away!
Now come on, save them today!

Omar Ouhaddou

Horrible Humans

Orangutans are dying away.
Rally and rumble to save them today.
A bunch of people are cutting down trees and those
Naughty people have to stop.
Grass and trees come crashing down.
U humans are horrible.
The orangutans run away.
All animals are running away!
Now come on, save them today!

Kaiden McGirr

Naught People

Orangutans are dying away.
Rally and rumble to save them today.
Animals are dying with
Naughty people cutting down trees.
Go and save the orangutan.
Up the trees they hide.
The animals never live.
Animals are running away!
Now come on, save them today!

Celia Mohamed

Terrifying

Orangutans are dying away.
Rally and rumble to save them today.
Animals are running away!
Now come on, save them today!
Giant trees are being cut down.
Up in the trees they hide while
Terrifying people are cutting them down.
Animals are running away!
Now come on, save them today!

Aiza Ahmed

Orangutans

Orangutans are dying away.
Really!
Animals climb on the trees.
Naughty monkey can mess the girl's room.
Get out silly monkey right now!
U are so crazy monkey.
The silly monkeys don't love me.
Animals are running away
Now come on and save the day!

Jury Al-Jabir

Get Out!

Orangutans are dying away.
Rally and rumble to save them today.
Animals are running away
Now help them today!
Get out our home!
U must go away!
This is our home!
Animals are running away!
Now come on, save them today!

Aleksander Kleszcz

Orangutan

Orangutans are dying away.
Rally and rumble to save them today.
An orangutan needs a home so
Now the humans have to stop, immediately!
Go away, naughty, bad humans!
Up the trees they hide.
The orangutans are hungry.
Animals are running away!
Now come on, save them today!

Nefera Barlow

Protection

Orangutans are dying away.
Rally and rumble to save them today.
All the naughty humans are chopping down trees so
Now we need to save them all.
Go away horrible humans.
Up the hyper animals go,
To all the other orangutans, protect your babies!
Animals are running away!
Now come on, save them today!

Sophia Fenjaly

Orangutan

Orangutans are dying away.
Rally and rumble to save them today.
All the orangutans are running.
Now come on and rescue them.
Go away naughty humans.
Up the trees we hide.
The humans have to stop.
Animals are running away!
Now come on, save them today!

Aisha Fahal

Why didn't you tell me?

Orangutan red.
Red is for anger.
And why didn't you tell me?
Now I am sad.
Go to safety.
Up the trees they quickly hide.
They humans might see us!
Animals are running away!
Now come on, save them today!

Jayden Chircop

Alive

Orangutans are dying away.
Rally and rumble to save them today.
Animals want to be alive but
Naughty humans like to cut down trees.
Giant trees are being chopped down!
U can't break any more trees because
The rainforest is not for humans.
Animals are running away!
Now come on, save them today!

Sara Talidi El Haddad

Go Away!

Orangutans are dying away.
Rally and rumble to save them today.
A girl is trusted to save the animals.
Naughty humans chop down the trees.
Go away!
Up the trees they hide.
The animals are dying.
Animals are running away!
Now come on, save them today!

Poppy Petrushkin

Swing Free

Orangutans swing freely through the trees
Reaching for branches
And vines that
No human has seen for thousands of years.
Grabbing for the branches
Under the canopy,
They are blissfully unaware of the impending doom
As humans chop their homes away, edging
Nearer to their idyllic homes.

Mr Pile

Orangutan

Orangutans are dying away.
Rally and rumble to save them today.
Animals are running from others.
No you can't stay in the rainforest humans!
Grass and trees are getting cut down.
U are horrible humans!
The orangutans are saving themselves by climbing trees.
Animals are running away!
Now come on, save them today!

Ayman Qassim

Hampstead
Year Two

Keeping the
World clean

Dirty Apple

On my way to Queen's Park I saw an apple.
I was a dirty apple.
It was a gross dirty apple.
It was a a muddy gross dirty apple.
It was a smelly, muddy, gross dirty apple.
It was a yucky, smelly, muddy, gross dirty apple.
So I threw it in the bin.

Rayan Hadidi

Dirty Bottle

On my way to Grandpa's house I saw a bottle.
It was a dirty bottle.
It was a shiny, dirty bottle.
It was a disgusting, shiny, dirty bottle.
It was a smelly, disgusting, shiny, dirty bottle.
So I put it in the bin

Alfie Dalton

Red Can

On my way to the mosque I saw a can.
It was a red can.
It was a red, wet can.
It was a shiny, red, wet can.
It was a disgusting, shiny, red, wet can.
It was an ugly, disgusting, shiny, red, wet can.
So I picked it up and put it in the bin.

Samara Rauf

Yellow Ice Cream Cone

On my way to Brent Cross I saw an ice cream cone.
It was a yellow ice cream cone.
It was a broken, yellow ice cream cone.
It was a disgusting broken, yellow ice cream cone.
It was an empty, disgusting, broken, yellow ice cream cone.
So I picked it up and put it in the bin.

Salman Yassin

Green Pear

On my way to school I saw a pear.
It was a green pear.
It was a smelly, green pear.
It was an old, smelly, green pear.
It was a disgusting, old, smelly, green pear.
So I picked it up and threw it in the bin.

Sumaya Ahmed

Candy Wrapper

On my way to Lidl I saw a candy wrapper.
It was a pink candy wrapper.
It was a dirty, pink candy wrapper.
It was a shiny, dirty, pink candy wrapper.
It was a sparkly, shiny, dirty, pink candy wrapper.
So I threw it in the smelly bin.

Emily Wintz

Bottle

On my way to Brent Cross I saw a bottle.
It was a smelly bottle.
It was a dirty, smelly bottle.
It was a slimy, dirty, smelly bottle.
So I threw it in the bin.

Asmaa Hassan

Can

On my way to the park I saw a can.
It was a dirty can.
It was a red, dirty can.
It was a wet, red, dirty can.
It was a broken, wet, red, dirty can.
So I picked it up and threw it in the bin.

Jana Mereu

Milkshake

On my way to McDonald's I saw a milkshake.
It was a smelly milkshake.
It was a rusty, smelly milkshake.
It was a squashed, rusty, smelly milkshake.
It was a red, squashed, rusty, smelly milkshake.
So I picked it up and put it in the rubbish bin.

Safiyyah Hussain

Bottle

On my way to Maya's house I saw a bottle.
It was an empty bottle.
It was a dirty, empty bottle.
It was a short, dirty, empty bottle.
So I picked it up and put it in the bin.

Zehra Mirza

Box

On my way to Queen's Park I saw a box.
It was a juice box.
It was a smashed juice box.
It was a dirty, smashed juice box.
It was a slimy, dirty, smashed juice box.
It was an empty, slimy, dirty, smashed juice box.
So I picked it up and I threw it in the bin.

Maya Bairli

Dawud

On my way to Green Park I saw a can.
It was a flat can.
It was sticky, flat can.
It was dirty, sticky, flat can.
It was slimy, dirty, sticky, flat can.
So I dumped it in the bin.

Dawud Hassan

Bottle

On my way to Hampstead Park I saw a bottle.
It was a plastic bottle.
It was a disgusting plastic bottle.
It was an ugly, disgusting plastic bottle.
It was a rusty, ugly, disgusting plastic bottle.
It was a slimy, rusty, ugly, disgusting plastic bottle.
So I picked it up and threw it in the blue bins.

Athaliah Singh

Box

On my way to school I saw a box.
It was a big box.
It was a smelly, big box.
It was a stinky, smelly, big box.
It was a disgusting, stinky, smelly, big box.
It was an ugly, disgusting, stinky, smelly, big box.
So I picked it up and put it in the bin.

Yazan Alkoud

Can

On my way to the park I saw a can
It was a smelly can.
It was a shiny, smelly can.
It was a squashed, shiny, smelly can.
It was a yucky, squashed, shiny, smelly can.
So I picked it up and put it in the bin.

Annie Stokes

Can

On my way to Hamleys I saw a can.
It was a disgusting can.
It was a dirty disgusting can.
It was a red, dirty disgusting can.
It was an ugly, red, dirty disgusting can.
So on my way to school I put it in the bin.

Yuften Hamza

Bottle

On my way to Lidl I saw a bottle.
I saw a smelly bottle.
I saw a slimy, smelly bottle.
I saw a dirty, slimy, smelly bottle.
So I picked it up and threw it in the bin.

Lina Ouadam

Can

On my way to the swimming pool I saw a can.
It was a gross can.
It was a rusty, gross can.
It was a shiny, rusty, gross can.
It was a smashed, shiny, rusty, gross can.
It was a broken, smashed, shiny, rusty, gross can.
So I picked it up and put it in the bin.

Kevin Gruev

Juice Box

On my way to Flip Out I saw a juice box.
It was an apple juice box.
It was a silver apple juice box.
It was a disgusting, silver apple juice box.
It was a smashed, disgusting, silver apple juice box.
So I put it in the bin.

Zekiah Chukwuka

Bottle

On my way to Flip Out I saw a bottle.
It was a dirty water bottle.
It was a yucky, dirty water bottle.
It was an ugly, yucky, dirty water bottle.
So I picked it up and then I threw it in the bin.

Amir Manna

Tin

On my way to Westfield, I saw a tin.
It was a slimy tin.
It was a smelly, slimy tin.
It was a wet, smelly, slimy tin.
So I picked it up and dumped it in the bin.

Mira Oueslati

Bottle

On my way to Brent Cross I saw a bottle.
It was a gross bottle.
It was a smelly, gross bottle.
It was a dirty, smelly, gross bottle.
So I picked it up and put it in the bin.

Jad Bassal

Juice Box

On my way to the beach I saw a juice box.
It was a smelly juice box.
It was a disgusting, smelly juice box.
It was a wet, disgusting, smelly juice box.
It was an orange, wet, disgusting, smelly juice box.
So I picked it up and threw it in the bin.

Maria Alwadi

Apple

On my way to school I saw an apple.
It was a broken apple.
It was an ugly, broken apple.
It was a slimy, ugly, broken apple.
It was a smelly, slimy, ugly, broken apple.
So I threw it away.

Ryanna Borzos

Bottle

On my way to Dawud's house I saw a bottle.
It was a juice bottle.
It was a gross, juice bottle.
It was a smelly, gross, juice bottle.
It was a rusty, smelly, gross, juice bottle.
It was an empty, rusty, smelly, gross, juice bottle.
It was a flat, empty, rusty, smelly, gross, juice bottle.
So I gave it to the rubbish man.

Sophie Chirac

Alexandra
Year Three

Saving the
Rainforests

I'm an Orangutan

I can feel my heart
Beating like a drum.
I can see the humans
Chopping the trees,
Killing the animals.
There's an apocalypse.
I can hear the animals
Screeching and screaming.
They're being dragged to their cage.
I can hear trees
Hurtling towards the ground.
I'm scared.
Am I about to die?

Anastasiya Fedoseyeva

My World

The world is going to die if we keep on going.
That's not all;
Heatwaves and climate change. Wow that change!
Talking about weather and droughts
That's not all;
Icebergs melting and forest fires destroying
Our world is in DANGER.
We need to look after our world.

Sulaiman Baida Benalal

46

I am an Orangutan

Animals dying in the forest.
Trees falling down tremendously.
Smoke coming ferociously like death is near.
Fire crackling and trees crashing.
My whole body trembling like an earthquake.
Why are these scary monsters destroying my home?

Adam Al-Ali

I'm an Endangered Orangutan

Fire leaving a trail of dead animals
Dangerous diggers erasing the forest
Smoke creeping wickedly through my home
Trees cracking and crumbling to the ground
Billowing smoke produced by the blazing fire
Humans made this into a different place.

Francesco Nunziata

Save The Forest

Trucks destroying my home.
Smoke devouring everything in its path.
Animals screeching in terror.
Animals are endangered.
Habitats are disappearing.
A human apocalypse is taking over.

Bahia Sande

I'm an Orangutan

I can smell smoke creeping through the air slowly.
I can feel fire burning my heart.
I can see fire spreading rapidly through the rainforest.
I can taste sweat dripping slowly down my face.
I can hear animals shrieking for help.
Why are the horrible humans destroying my home?

Omar Blaaza

Save My Home

I can see the sky as red as a blood moon.
I can smell trees being burnt.
I can hear dangerous bulldozers coming closer every single second.
I can hear fire crackling furiously.
I can smell horrifying smoke in the air.
I can see it billowing as high as the sky.

Riyad Boudal Moumni

Save my Forest

I see trees,
But my forest is broken.
I can hear animals running.
I can smell deathly smoke.
I can see fire coming towards me.
I can taste sweat dripping down my face.
I can feel death is coming.

Ali Al Dhatiry

48

Save My Forest

I can see fire coming towards me.
I can see a truck dragging my mother away.
I can smell burning trees.
I can smell dirty smoke in the air.
I can hear baby animals screaming.
I can hear fire crackling.
The humans are killing my family.

Tasnim Dekhissi

Save My Forest

I can see the fire burning trees.
I can hear them falling down.
I can smell the fire blazing.
I can feel hot fire coming closer.
The humans are destroying my home.

Sally Alhamadani

Save My Forest

I can see trees falling down.
I can hear animals crying.
I can smell fire is burning.
I can feel hot fire coming towards me.
The humans crushing my trees.

Sondas Aldahi

Save My Forest

I can see trees on the ground.
I can see smoke creeping to the sky.
I can smell burning trees.
I can feel a hot fire.
I can hear bulldozers cutting trees.

Hamany Ali

Save My Forest

Fire is rushing through the trees
Like the animals who are risking their lives.
Smoke is creeping into the trees
Like the baby animals looking for their family.
My heart is pounding
Like the animals sprinting to save their lives.
And just as I touch the grass
it fades away to nothing.

Emily Fowkes

Human Apocalypse

Bulldozers wrecking my home carelessly.
Monsters tearing my trees ruthlessly from the ground.
Smoke billowing like it has no mind.
Fire blazing menacingly through the forest.
I'm watching helplessly as my world disappears.

Dean Hussain

I'm An Orangutan

Fire crackling wickedly like a furious volcano;
The sky is as red as a blood moon.
Animals risking their lives to save their young.
Burned trees turned to ashes.
Outrageous diggers ripping trees apart like monstrous buffaloes.
Haunted bulldozers wrecking our home.
What did we do to deserve this?

Fabian-Nohr Buchanan

Human Apocalypse

Fire burning as hot as a volcano.
Smoke spreading rapidly.
Diggers digging as annoying as a concert while you are asleep.
My body trembling like an earthquake.
Animals running faster than a cheetah
Desperately trying to escape.

Babaker Mohamedkhair

Human Apocalypse

The bulldozers wrecking the trees ruthlessly.
Deadly smoke passing me by.
Never ending screams from the young of my family,
The ground shaking as the bulldozers approach.
Animals running for their lives,
Running from this horrifying human apocalypse.

Mumin Babar

Save my Forest

I can see towering trees.
I can smell burning hot smoke.
I can hear horrifying diggers.
I can feel hot fire coming towards me.

Shaelah Hassan

I am an Orangutan

The moon is as red as blood.
I see bulldozers destroying my home.
I hear animals shrieking like a fire alarm.
I feel my heart pounding rapidly.
Trees apart, animals risking their lives.
I smell smoke creeping wickedly through the trees.
I can smell burnt trees turned into ashes.
I can hear fire crackling ferociously.
Blazing hot fire blasting and bashing on the trees.
Blood of the animals dripping as the shower goes on.

Ayeza Sheikh

Save the Forest

I can see red fire.
I can hear crunching trees.
I can smell smoke in the air.
I can feel my heart beating.
The humans are destroying my home.

Ibrahim Qureshi

I am an Orangutan

I can see animals dying like a blood moon.
I can hear the trucks crushing the trees.
I can taste my sweat.
I can smell smoke.
I can feel my heart beating fast.
I can taste smoke inside my mouth.
I can see next to me, trees breaking down.
I can feel fire burning the trees.
I can feel fire next to me.

Muhammed Elfruh

Help Me and the Forest

I can see fire blazing.
I can hear diggers chopping wood.
I can smell smoke.
I can feel my heart beating.

Hyusein Basko

My Precious Home

Trees being burnt,
Cracking from the trees.
Dirty smoke in the air,
My body shaking from fear.
Why are these humans destroying my precious home?

Lorenc Miha

Falling Trees

I can see fire hot as the flaming sun.
I can smell smoke choking me.
I can hear trees falling down like big trucks crashing.
I can touch trucks grabbing the trees like a hurricane.

Jaydah Roberts

My Home is Destroyed

I can see fire dancing in the smoky sky.
I can hear the screams of the horrified animals.
I can smell the dirty smoke in the air billowing furiously.
I can taste sweat trickling down my face and into my mouth.
I can see bulldozers obliterating my home.

Leila Boukrouh

Mapesbury
Year Three

Deforestation

Smoky Gun

Tall trees falling down.
Mud all over my body.
Burning fire blasting all around me.
Smoky gun bullets shooting rapidly.
Heat burning my hands.

Rawad Alenizi

Towering Trees

Towering tall trees being chopped down.
Strong powerful flames,
Crackling fire,
Dirty smoke in my body.

Adnan Al Dhatiry

Monsters

They are cutting the trees like monsters.
Enormous bulldozers destroying my home.
Blood in my mouth,
Toxic smoke killing me,
Help!

Rayan Rafik

Giant

Trees crashing on the floor in a big stomp like a giant
Smoke burning the big trees
Broken

Jaanvi Mandalia

Deforestation

Heat
Toxic smoke
Trees falling
Trees burning
Blood dripping
Humans

Mohamad Kounbas

Breath

Bulldozers point as sharp as razors,
Trees slamming and falling from the sky.
Fire burning,
Soot everywhere,
Trees sawed to stumps like a piece of crisp.
I can taste smoke and I can't breathe.

Jonathan Bruma

Deforestation

Dark smoke spreading slowly all around the fire.
Flames of burning trees
Dirty plants splattering on me.
Loud explosions banging my eardrums,
Smoke choking me

Rianne Dahaymeesh

Wrecking Balls

Wrecking balls clang aggressively,
Debris scratching my body.
Blood drooling out of my mouth.
Friends slowly losing their lives.

Solayman Moujahid

Deforestation

I can see snapping trees.
I can hear scary loud gunshots.
I can smell rotten air.
I can taste the damp.
I can feel the heat of the burning fire.

Theo Merlin

Crackling

I can see some chopped down trees.
I can hear a crackling fire.
I can touch the fallen snapped trees.
I can taste the rotten stale smoke.

Kairo Manning

Home

Wrecking balls firing explosions
Dirty mud and melting grass
Sweat dripping
Toxic smoke poisoning us
Humans are destroying my forest
My home.

Nadine Valani Kloss

I can

I can smell burning smoke.
I can taste fire.
I can hear a bulldozer.
I can see chopped down trees.
I can feel everything falling on me.

Brooklyn Forrest

Demolished

Burning grass as black as coal,
Smoke from deadly dynamite everywhere.
Clangs like a wrecking ball clashing into a giant building being
Demolished.
Twigs as sharp as knives piercing into my body;
Smoke ripping my throat as I try to survive.

Affan Asif

Deforestation

I can see burning fumes.
I can smell toxic smoke.
I can hear loud noises.
I can feel heat blasting.
I can taste my blood.

Saidomar Hasan

Heartbroken

A crane as giant as a mountain killing destructively.
Burning smoke, growing slowly, choking all animals without care.
Indestructible sharp blades slicing my home.
Thick, rough wood exploding,
Salty blood dripping slowly,
Breaking my heart.

Haadi Hussain

Deforestation

A crane cuts down trees in the forest taking palm oil.
Machines crush trees and bash everything, everywhere.
Burning fire destroys my home.
I can taste blood drooling my mouth.
Tears dripping down my face.

Hannah Failey

Escape

I can see the deadly dark.
I can smell burning fire.
I can hear a loud explosion.
I can taste dirty powerful smoke.
I can feel the moist ground.
I need to escape.

Aseel Alhamadani

Death

Burning fire bursting through the forest.
Like gunshots flying in the air.
Flaming tree-wood burns me.
Choking smoke.
My family is dying.

Sami Fumagalli

Misery

The cranes are eating the mud like angry monsters.
The forest floor shakes like a volcano erupting.
The sky is miserable and black like coal.
The toxic gas burns from the tip of my nose.
The dirty smoke is poisoning my body.

Stefana Morosanu

Deforestation

Smoke like a cigarette.
Bulldozers clanging.
Chopped down trees as hard as cement.
Burnt homes with fires blazing.
Animals fearfully running and screaming.
I'm choking on my last breath.

Carly Barcenas Pradhan

Sensing Destruction

I can see lots of broken down trees on the ground; an abandoned forest.
I can hear an enormous rattle like an earthquake.
I can feel the burning heat of fire like the hot sun.
I can smell erupting fire like an exploding volcano.
I can taste tears miserably like the salty ocean.

Amina Sobirkhonova

Deforestation

Bulldozers as mammoth as a mountain.
Dead trees in a smoke cloud.
Sky-high trees crashing the ground like giants stomping the floor.
Burning plants.
Puffy smoke as dirty as the bottom of a shoe.

Benedicte Kassi

What I Can

I can see burning smoke shooting across the sky.
I can see them cutting down the tall trees and that makes me sad.
I can smell burning smoke.
I can hear the tall trees falling down.
I can feel the loud trucks.
I can taste the wet leaves.

Karam Faroukh

Desparation

Fire burning the forest floor.
Wrecking balls destroying my home.
Dark smoke against me.
I am desperate.

Aishya Holmes

Battersea
Year Four

Our World

Save the World

The fire is red as blood,

The fire glowing like lava,

The fire flaring up into the sky.

The fire is alive!

The trees reach out above the fire.

The leaves change colour.

The leaves fall down to the ground.

Save our trees!

By

Ana Todor, Anthony Stokes, Nyla Wilmott, Rimas Aldandan,
Taqwa Rashedi

Trees

The trees are big.

The trees are beautiful.

Stop cutting

Our trees down.

If we carry on like this

The Earth will die.

By Madina Mamadjonova

Our Fading Rainforests

The rainforests are very bright,

It's such a lovely sight!

The smells, sounds and colours

Will soon all be a memory,

Even you and me.

Deforestation

Is destroying Earth's foundation.

We humans are greedy.

Animals are dying.

Now that forests are gone,

Children are crying.

SAVE OUR WORLD

by Phoebe Savage

Animals

All the plastic in the sea,

It's killing the fish

And we are killing the bees.

All the animals

Are becoming extinct.

We need to stop

Putting animals in exhibits.

We need to stop

Doing everything for money.

We need bees for honey.

We use and abuse animals.

What we should really do is …

SAVE OUR WORLD

by Reign Richards

STOP!

People are using oil to make plastic;

So stop!

People are cutting down trees for paper;

So stop!

Using fossil fuel, taking long showers to cool,

Using up water in their swimming pool.

Just stop!

People are killing our animals;

So stop!

People are ruining our oceans;

So stop!

Chopping down trees, polluting our seas, killing our bees.

Just stop!

by Muhammad Mudabir

Animals

Animals are in danger.

Narwhals are nearly extinct.

Irrawaddy Dolphins are nearly extinct.

Mountain gorillas are nearly extinct

All animals will be extinct in a few years.

Look after our world.

Save our animals.

Amelia Rabbani

Help the World

Stop using plastic.

Help the world.

Stop killing nature.

Help the world.

Start turning off lights,

Give animals their rights.

Stop ruining our planet.

Help the world.

by Maya Puzuk

Our Environment

Our world is in danger

Because of our greed.

Greedy companies cut down trees

For money.

Greedy humans drill for oil,

Dig for coal,

For money.

Greedy people make plastic –

So much plastic –

For money.

But they, **we**,

Could still make money

Without ruining nature,

Without destroying our planet.

by Luca Morosanu

Those Luscious Green Leaves

A tree stands in the wild

With those luscious green leaves.

A trunk as strong as stone

With flowers to feed the bees.

One day,

When the leaves were glimmering

And the sun was shimmering

And warm,

There was a man

Who came to

Chop down the tree.

And so it began:

The end of the world.

by Dilys Jones

Nature

Now stop destroying our world.

At this moment we can't carry on.

Today, lots of our plants are gone.

Use things that don't harm our Earth.

Right now we can still help our plants.

Everybody can help us help the world.

Adnan Jaabak

Environment

If we carry on like this,

Throwing plastic away,

The world we know

Will end.

Our animals and plants

Are dying.

Humans will soon

Die too.

Let's worry about what matters:

Love,

Knowledge,

Kindness,

Friendship.

Not plastic!

by Omar Ahmad

Save the World

I can't imagine Mother Earth

Without God's creatures

Such diversity

So interdependent

They need all of us

We need all of them

I cannot imagine Mother Earth

Without God's creatures

by Griffin Dias

Plastic

People think that plastic is OK

But it's not;

It's choking our seas, fish are dying.

Animal habitats have vanished

Because of everything we're doing.

If we carry on like this

All that will be left is

All the treasures of the world

Buried underground

And plastic covering them.

The world is warning us to stop.

WE NEED TO STOP.

Plastic is not OK!

by Victoria Corrazzin

Start to Make a Change

Pass this message on:

Love our planet

All that plastic

Suffocating the seas.

The world does not need plastic.

It's costing up the Earth.

Crusade with us.

Stop using plastic!

Maryam Khan

The Beauty of the Amazon

The Amazon: The lungs of the Earth.

The beautiful sunset and horizon

Spreads through this luscious rainforest.

The limpid water shines

As the sun rises.

The mint green leaves

Grow on the trees.

But the Amazon is not as lovely as before:

Because of chopping down trees

And destroying habitats

And trapping animals.

Only if we stop will the Amazon

Be like it was before.

by Kyalsin Myint

Waste

StoP using plastic!

All that Litter

All that wAste

Single use Selfishness

PolluTing our seas

Killing our anImals

But we can Change all that!

by Temple Joseph

Plants Acrostic

Please respect our plants

Their **L**eaves provide food and shelter

They **A**llow us to breathe

They give us **N**utrients

They give us frui**T**s

They are key to our **S**urvival

By Ahmed Zeeshan

Nature Fights Back

We must act **N**ow

Our world is in the **A**utumn of its life

The **T**rees are disappearing

Poll**U**tion invades our seas

Sto**R**ms are increasing

The **E**arth is dying

Re**F**orestation

Winds f**I**ghting back

Stop litterin**G**; it's polluting the Earth

Help nurture plants

Stop defores**T**ation

Use **S**olar energy

Before it's too late

We need to think **A**bout what matters

About what **C**ounts

Before we **K**ill our Earth

by Sibel Karayusein

Animals

Animals are dying

HuNted to extinction

Their habItats destroyed

Monstrous cages trapping them

Their food contAminated

Their air poLluted

Stop this now!

by Samir Afrangi

Nature

Stop destroying our home
With plastic,
Lots of plastic.
It is surrounding
The Earth.
We are killing animals,
And fish
With all the plastic
We throw in the sea.
They are being tangled
And strangled.
We need to stop
Before it's too late!

by Afreen

Victoria
Year Four

Saving Earth

Climate Change

They're destroying the forest and the cracking of the Earth below,
Animals are hopeless and running out of habitats.
Just because of humans needing palm oil.
We will never find a planet B.
We can't replace planet A.

Species are dying and in fear of gunshots.
Animals need our help!
We need to do even more,
To keep the beautiful rainforest floor.

We will regret chopping trees,
When there is no rainforest left.
Animals gone forever so many species are dead.
We are going to be full of regret.

Sea levels are rising with raging waves,
Ice caps are melting, sending animals to their graves.
We need to do even more,
To save the ocean and rainforest floor.

Suraya Yasin

Climate change

Gorillas running for their lives from the raging fire,
Birds are flying higher and higher.
We live on a planet we must protect,
If we don't we will be full of regret.

Many species are dying
And some governments are lying,
Sea levels are rising,
The animals and the rainforests continue dying.

We can't go back in time,
So let's begin to change the rhyme.
Plants are dying we need to be kind
And clever like Einstein,

Stop using palm oil and
Stop using car oil.
Get an electric car instead.
Or this planet will be dead.

Climate change!
Change the climate.

Azhar Mahamed

Protect our Planet

We live on a planet we must protect.
If we don't, we will be full of regret.
Many species are dying, and the government is lying.
We can't go back in time so let's change the rhyme.
Animals are dying and while humans are thriving.
Stop buying products with palm oil,
Do your bit to save the soil.

Kayden Mooney

Tiger

I see a big tiger
Here in the zoo.
He needs somewhere bigger
Than this cage
It is true.
He is lying down,
And
Looking very blue.

Rimas Kanbas
Lily Kbies
Mubarek Aman

Four Reasons to Save our Planet

Small brown monkeys swooshing through inferno fire,
While red pandas barely escape
From similar danger
From traps left by us.

Sharks are dying,
They used to thriving
As an apex predator
In oceans and seas.
So give them some ease with the shark fin soup.

Towering trees strike the forest floor at
Hypersonic speed,

We need to save our planet as there is nowhere else
For us to go.

Icebergs melting, polar bears floating out in the ocean left to die.
Avalanches falling more and more often in those
Frozen lands.
Temperature is getting warmer
The earth is being destroyed.
Second by second,
Minute by minute,
Hour by hour

The Earth will soon be no more.

Sulayman Hussain

Protect Them

Brown muddy monkeys swooshing past the inferno fire,
While the red pandas are escaping from the crazy, wildfire.

Large black and white pandas eating bamboo,
As the inferno fire spreads on the forest floor.

Enormous gorillas swiftly sprinting away from the raging flames,
Trying to the bulldozers rolling down from the hill tops to destroy
their habitats even more.

Lonely large tigers, their numbers are falling,
So many of them are slowly dying.
Hunted and killed by horrible humans,
With no care for life or species facing extinction.

Haikal Afandi

Climate Change

Everyone can stop nature from dying,
Everyday our animals are crying!
We live on a planet we must protect,
If we don't we will be full of regret.

We must stay strong, true and loyal,
Let's make a promise to use less palm oil!
Animals are dying because of humankind
be clever like Einstein.

Rescue animals big and small,
Rescue animals short and tall.
Animals need helping and icecaps are melting!

Trees are crashing down
Animals are staring at their homes on the ground.
You can see, there is no planet B.

Gorillas are roaming out of their homes,
Can you hear the animals moan?
You can see, there is no planet B.

Polar bears are dying
and parakeets are crying!
You can see there is no planet B!

We can help.
Do you hear our animals yelp?
Eat more vegetables, eat less meat.
You can see there is no planet B!

Robin–Ameen Buchanan

Climate change

A great big crashing waterfall, whooshing parakeets,
palm trees with big beautiful branches, I can really feel the heat.
But then I look behind me as the evil wood trucks drive
I scream "NO!" and soon they go but they will be back for more.

A great big crashing waterfall, whooshing parakeets,
I realise now we have to vow that we'll save the broken planet.

Act now to save tomorrow,
Or we will be forever left in sorrow.
To Earth we must be loyal,
And make a pledge to use less palm oil.

Work hard to plant trees,
Put less plastic in our seas,
Grow your own food, it's free!
It will help pollinator bees.

A brilliant blue sky is what we want to see,
Not a grey polluted sky with a CRASHING fallen down tree.

A great big crashing waterfall, whooshing parakeets,
Palm trees with big beautiful branches, I can really feel the heat.

This is the world we want so we must work hard for it,
To save our broken planet, you won't regret it a bit.

Jessica Mailer

Animals

Animals worried and terrified,
They need our help.
Save the world.

We must fight to keep animals safe and sound
So they will not be afraid.

River's fading away,
Poor animals habitats destroyed.
Animals, trees, plants and rivers disappearing.

Rafif Dahaymeesh

Human in my Forest

There is a human in my forest and I don't know what to do,
He took away my family and I'm scared he'll take me too.
There is a human in my forest and I don't know what to do,
They cut down trees for palm oil for humans to use.

There is a human in my forest and I don't know what to do,
He took away my family and put them in the zoo.
There is a human in my forest and I don't know what to do,
He took away my family and I am scared they'll take me too.

Moustafa Elsayed Moustafa Ibrahim Ali

Save Our Planet

Defenceless, gigantic animals crying,
As the planet is dying day by day.
If we don't help we will pay.
We need to help instead of sitting down all day.

Sea levels are rising higher and higher.
Only we can stop the fire
That's raging all around.
Only we can help the planet,
Make it brighter.

We are lucky we aren't those defenceless animals
Crying
Day and night.
Only we can make the planet brighter
We must put up a bigger fight!

Haris Darr

Climate Change

The massive iceberg melting the homes,
The polar bears are crying and all alone.
Let's stop climate change,
Before we regret the damage to this beautiful place.

Tigers losing their babies and are scared.
Tigers are begging for help can you do that for them?
Let's stop climate change,
before we regret the damage to this beautiful place.

Species becoming endangered, dying out so quickly,
They don't know what is happening, their lives are destroyed .
Let's stop climate change,
before we regret the damage to this beautiful place.

Noorhan Hamdi

Make Nature Happy

The tall towering trees dying from the raging fire,
all the red pandas crying while animals are dying.
Hearing them crying makes it terrifying.

Parrot are flying to get away from the deadly forest
Gorillas are running away from the fires.
Animals are losing homes food,
It leaves them in an awful mood.

When we make nature happy,
The animals around us become safe.

Rafif Alfrwh

Regret

Gorillas and Orangutan running from burning fire
And birds are flying higher and higher.
The animals are running for their lives
And humans are cutting with their knives.

We live on a planet we must protect,
If we don't we will regret.

You have to try to stop using palm oil.
People are taking Orangutan's homes
All they're leaving are piles of bones.
Taking away families and putting them in cages
Locked up for ages and ages.
The animals are dying,
And the animals are crying.

We live on a planet we must protect,
If we don't we will regret.

Hafsa Choudhury

Save Them

Pandas are crying, wiping their tears,
We needs to help them before it's too late.

Countless orangutans running from danger,
Many people line up for hire.
Because of all that greed and money,
There can be no harmony.

We won't be able to live with this,
It may lead to an apocalypse.
So please don't make nature hide,
Or else earth will turn to its bad side.

Ice caps falling because of temperatures rising,
Resulting in hopeless polar bears crawling,
White rhinos are the most hated albinos,
Because humans keep on using weapons
To snap off their massive bony horns!

So please try to be the most earth friendly,
It can and will make a giant difference.
Stop the deforestation;
It is a very bad consequence.

Seve Hefferon

Our Planet

We have a planet that we live on and it's in danger,
Because of us.
Tigers are racing through the dying forest,
And the parrots are squawking in pain.
The orangutans are trapped in cages.

Trees are thundering right to the forest floor.
Palm trees being chopped down just for oil.
Gorillas being killed and other terrible things coming.

Let's make a change before it's too late.
We must tell the government to stop deforestation,
Let's work together to save our Earth and nation.

Malaak Ali

Deforestation

Red pandas are dying, animals are crying.
Inferno fires are killing too many animals,
Deforestation is destroying the rainforests.
Animals don't deserve live like this,
They should be living in harmony and bliss.

Peacocks are dying, animals are whining.
Deforestation must be stopped.
Animals don't deserve live like this,
They should be living in harmony and bliss.

Lola Alexander Murphy

Planet A

Trees are falling like
Dominoes and smoke is
Rising quick as a flash.

There is no planet B,
So cherish this one we see.

Fires are thriving,
And forests are dying,
Almost as if they were never there.

There is no planet B,
So cherish this one we see.

Plop go the icecaps and
Puff go the penguins, polar
Bears, narwhals and fish.
But we can save them,
If we want to.

There is no planet B,
So cherish this one we see.

Hurricanes and forest fires
Are now no longer rare.
Humans just don't even seem to care.

There is no planet B,
So cherish this one we see.

George Fazzini

No Planet B

There is no planet B,
So cherish this one we see.

Trees are crashing down like dominoes,
We can help the animals and their homes,
Before they are fully destroyed.

Turn off the light switch,
Turn down the lamp,
Before you turn off the Earth.

People are chopping down and
Destroying forests,
Animals running away
From danger.

We want a bright,
Blue sky
Like blue blossoms.

Help the world.

Help the birds before they have to stop flying.
Animals everywhere are just dying and dying.

This poem is now finished.
But did you get my message?
We must stop climate change.

Scarlett John-Baptiste

Protect our Planet

Beautiful birds fluttering over the raging fire,
Red pandas habitats are being torn down.
There is nothing left on the ground!

Endangered animals lose their homes,
They then end up all alone.

We live on a planet we must protect,
If we don't we will regret.

Sea levels are rising,
Polar bears and penguins are left crying.
Listen to what I am saying,
Because animal homes are fading.

We live on a planet we must protect,
If we don't we will regret.

So many animal populations have shrunk,
So these beautiful creatures will be extinct.
Just a distant memory far back in our minds.

We live on a planet we must protect,
If we don't we will regret.

Sana Shakib

Deforestation

Animals are dying!
Bulldozers are thriving!

Gorillas are rapidly running,
To stay free from captivity.

Rainbow coloured parrots,
Flying from the monstrous bulldozers
Onto the treetop vines of freedom.

Our helpless
And defenceless
White rhinos are no more,
Because of human selfishness and greed.

Animals in our world are dying,
We must save them
And not
Let more species become extinct!

William Baloshi

Kensington
Year Five

Saving the
World

Save the Polar Bears

Polar bears have
Soft
White
Fur

And live on the freezing Ice cold ice caps.
They probably wish they had a jetpack to escape those icecaps.

Their families went
Back to their
Packs

To escape those icecaps.
They probably wish they had a pack of food to gorge on.

The ice caps are melting
We might dare to care.

Florian Ruether

Tigers

Tigers are endangered
In the forest is where they live
Growling at their prey
Eating tonnes of deer
Running away from poachers
Save them from extinction

Faisal Al-Kailani

Polar Bears

Pretty Fur
Others want us
Long live the polar bear.
Animals are beautiful
Run, they're coming!!

Big and furry
Extinction is coming!
All together we can do our part
Recycle more!!!

Elianna St. Rose

Gorillas

Gorillas like to eat bananas
Oranges are not their favourite fruit
Roaming and thumping their chests
In a forest is where they live
Lying down on a bed of grass and leaves
Lots and lots of family
All around them
Stop cutting down trees!

Daniil Buryi

Gorillas

Gorilla's have a fluffy back
Over five feet tall
Round the world they eat insects, bananas and leaves
Intruders burn the gorillas house
Leaders have the silver pack
Living in the forest
All the gorillas are nearly extinct

Malek El-Houry
Letlotlo Mokhutsoane

Nature

Trees are beautiful just like flowers,
They smell just like fresh air in my hair.

Trees help us to breath by giving us oxygen.
When people cut down trees
It gives us less oxygen every time.

If people cut down trees, just for paper
We should not waste it.
It's easy as pie to not waste paper.
Nature is trees
And it all around us.
We need to take care of trees
Or they will fall apart because of us.
We should promise that won't happen.

Kiarna Wildman

Gorillas

Gorilla, gorilla, gorilla that's the scientific name.
Of course they eat few bits of meat although they're omnivores.
Responsibility lies in the silverback for it is the leader.
Instead of living in trees, they live in nests on the ground.
Loving young till five months old.
Lovely flowers surrounds their nests.
And gorillas are apes, orangutans as well.
Saving trees means saving gorillas.

Helping hands are recycling more.
Only they are more friendly than other monkeys.
Monkeys have tail's gorillas don't have tails as a fact.
Every carnivore act as predators to gorillas.
Slithering snakes are under gorillas.

Animals are in danger because of poachers.
Responsibility is needed from humans.
Exit the forests and let them be.

Forest's are homes to gorillas.
Only forest's are smaller than the Amazon rainforest.
Rivers keep the gorilla's alive.
Essentials are just bugs, leaves and twigs.
Stop cutting down trees, they are for gorillas.
Trees give humans and animals life.
Save gorillas if you think you're kind.

Khadija Asif

Help the Trees

One by one each tree falls
One by one each animal leaves.
Until there is one tree left all alone.
The tree stands waiting until it falls down.
All alone there are no trees.
Trees are healthy and help us breathe.
Save the trees.

Hajara Namanda

Gorillas

Gorillas live in West Africa
Orphan gorillas all around
Recycle more to save their trees
Intruders are taking over their homes
Less and less food for us to eat
Listen to us and save our world
Air is giving to us by tree
Silverbacks are the leaders of the pack

Gerison Shehi

Animals

Recycle more.
Animals are dying.
If you can donate, do it!
No more killing animals.
Focus more on nature.
Oceans are important.
Raining is good for trees.
End cutting trees.
Save animals that are dying.
Today, care about nature!

Salman Mohamed

Terrified Tigers

So large fluffy orange and black,

The poachers have us under attack,

Our fur so precious,

On the back of the selfish

Why do they treat us like that?

£20,000! Who's the highest bidder?

How do we stop this crime?

If only it was as easy as calling 999!

Abdulkadir Mohamed, Maya Krikra, Anett Bodi

Gorillas

Gorillas like to eat bananas
Oranges are not their favourite
Roaring and thumping their chests
In a forest is where they live
Lying down on a bed of grass and leaves
Lots and lots of family
All around them
Stop cutting down trees!

Arina Tsybulko

Nature is in Danger

Nature is in danger
Air comes from trees
Trees are important for gorillas and oxygen
Understand nature, we might not have it in the future
Rainforests are in danger
Earth is being damaged

If you ever find a dead polar bear, never eat its liver
Nature belongs to animals and people are damaging nature.

Day by day animals are dying and getting out of food
Animals are dying but people don't care
Nature is really important for everyone not just for animals,
Gorillas are a part of nature so care for them not kill them
Earth is a part of nature don't waste paper recycle
Rainforests are in danger.

Rania Faisal

Rainforests

Rainforest are cut each year
Animals have a home in trees and we are taking them away
In the Amazon rainforest tribes are losing there homes
No more pollution in this world
Feathered friends live there
On top of you every day
Round the world there are animals
Every day animals lose their homes
Saving trees means saving animals
The trees are saving us but we are not saving them

Na'Idah Simba

Peace Forever

Rainforests are everywhere; let's leave them in their beauty
Animals need our help so let's do are duty
It's crazy how people like to cut them down
No one should do it without a frown
Faces of animals on the wall
Oceans are dying along with coral
Racing cheetahs running along the savannah
Excited poachers along with a hunter banner
Save the animals we'll do it together
Today we unite so animals can live in peace forever.

Robin Trippier

112

Gorillas

Furry, friendly, fierce gorillas roaming through the jungle.
Sometimes they can be funny, maybe even tumble.
Sometimes they can play fight
Whethere it's light or at night.
They have a loud chest thump,
Loud enough to make you jump.

With an average life span of about 35 years,
They're so brave they have zero fears.
These cute animals need a safe home
Or at least somewhere that they can roam

Rayan Kaisar

The Ugly Truth

Be careful of what you are buying
The animals are dying
Don't just sit there sighing
We need to start trying.

A hunter's glory
Is a good story
But it always gets gory.

A gorilla's life
Shouldn't end with a knife
Don't let them go to the light
Let's end the fight!

Eric Clarke

Trees

Taller than the tallest man on Earth
Reaching for the skies. It's
Easy to stop cutting them down but
Easy to suffer without them.
Stop cutting down trees.

Got to learn about nature
In all the rainforests. They are
Very old.
Even trees bleed

Living in all kind of places you'll find them
In the local woods where
Feathered friends are always welcome to roost a while.
Every day we use trees oxygen. So stop cutting down trees.

Afrah Amour

All About Gorillas

Gorillas are grey and dads are silverbacks.
They are as protective as a woman over her baby as a human.
Gorillas are kind and it's like they're blind.
Gorillas are large and they can charge really hard.
Gorillas can jump, but some are lazy.
Gorillas are mad when bad poachers destroy their homes.
Gorillas get sad when their family members die and they say
Goodbye.

Amira Ahmed

Endangered Animals

Some animals are endangered
Some are about to die.
I know it sounds impossible but this isn't a lie.
Ice caps are melting.
Trees are being cut down.
Please do your part.
So animals can stay safe and sound.

Tyler Sambo

Gorilla

I am a silverback and I lost my pack.
They're probably in cages
But I don't know that.
I am upset because they're probably in cages.
I lost their scent so
I don't know where they are.

Devontae Richards-Harris

Banana

Some animals are in danger and don't know how to trust a
stranger.
Polar bears, pandas and narwhals; if we don't play our part it will
break their heart.
Gorillas climb on trees and some eat leaves.
They greet each other with touch but don't talk much.
Gorillas walk on their arms but don't use their palms.

Aliya Fahal

Rainforest

Around the world there is danger.
Animals are being endangered.
In the world you can help it.
Nature is around us we can't let it go.
Forest are being cut down for farms.
Obey our rules to help within the world.
Respect these live they need you.
Earth is being destroyed because of you.
Save these animals lives.
They can bring you joy.
Tame these animals with braveness
Or help them reach vet.

Bahaa Issa

Hyde
Year Five

Rainforest
Reactions

Amazon rainforest

Amazon Rainforest
Magnificent rainforest
Amazon rainforest as calm as a sunny day
Zebra is like a Oreo
One beautiful Amazon
No destroying the Amazon rainforest

Rainforest with birds tweeting, leopards are growling
Amazon rainforest as noisy as a funfair
Iguana on branches
No cutting down trees
Fire burning the beautiful trees
Once again save the Amazon rainforest
Rainforest as cool as a rainy day
Emotional monkey crying for their mum
Slimy scary slippery snake
Take gorillas and give them a home

Hassan Imtiaz

The Amazon Rainforest

Amazing like the amusement park
Magnificent animals
Awesome animals
Zebras don't belong in zoos
Orange trees are the best
No cutting of nature allowed

Red panda are cute and clumsy
Adult tigers are ferocious
Instantly having fun with animals
Newts are cute
Forests are outstandings
Onyx are rare
Rainforests are calm and quiet
Exciting places
Slick tigers
Tempting us to go inside

Celine Fouani

Arctic Fox

As smart as a professor,
Rapid as a
Cheetah,
Tactical hearing before they get their food
Icy terrains they roam,
Cunning as a crow,

Fearfully hunted for a fluffy cushion,
Occasionally jumping in the snow for its food,
Xenial to its kits.

Leo Toumert

Arctic Wolf

Adorable and fluffy
Running faster than the wind
Casually
Trailing across the snow while
Ice melts across the planet endangering
Cold animals

Water wasted
Oppressed animals
Lovely endangered animals
Fearful, so leave them alone.

Chelsea Roberts

Breath by Breath

Amur leopards are stealthy beasts,
but still can't defend their home,
as poachers burn their habitat.

They run in the woods;
they don't know what's happening.

Bright lights,
gun shots
the smell of smoke.

Orange flames in the forest,
was all they know.

Trees dropping and cages unlocking,
Screams of family finally arrive,

Cars drifting.
Guns shooting.
More running.

Breath by breath,
the Amur leopard falls.

A gentle breeze sweeps across its face,
in the dawn.

Abdulaziz Ahmed

Gorilla

Gentle giant apes swinging through the tress of the jungle
Only a kind heart in a bog body
Roaming the jungle like a curious toddler
Intellingent but endangered
Lurking poachers waiting in the dark
Lazing and lying in the sun
Adventurous but helpless when danger faces them.

Arlo Petrushkin

Gorilla

Small species, gentle giants enjoying life as small as a baby

GORILLA

Destroyed habitats, never forgotten, beautiful babies, almost dead

GORILLA

Adorable animals, strong species smoky smell love them all

GORILLA

black grey, every colour you want raging fire, no more trees

GORILLA

Life of GORILLA is sad but if you want to do your part try

Ibrahim Hassan

Gorillas

Gentle giants
On the snowy mountains.
Ravaging fire
Inferno in their homes.
Long limbs,
Leaves, shoots and pith.
Aggressive but they are gentle healthy vegetarians,
Swinging in the trees.

Imran Mohammed

Red Panda Poem

Really good at climbing trees

Ever furry warm coats

Dawn and dusk, I look for food

Population of just 10,000

A long bushy tail wraps around like a blanket

Natural habitat of mountains and trees

Diet of bamboo, bird eggs and leaves

Asia is the place for me.

Aleeza Khan

Hurricane

It was a captivating day,
and everyday until today,
Hurricane Ian made its way.

It came from the
Arctic sea,
All the way to
Florida,
strolled and stumbled,
all the way to me.

It yelled and howled like
it was a wolf.
It twirled and wondered
skipped everywhere;
soon it will be roaming
like a bear.

Ian came closer
to me,
threw an object
at my head.
I passed out,
woke-up somewhere dusty.
I was dizzy, hungry and lonely
wondering if I'll die
today or in the next one.

Maryam Naeem

Panda

Pandas run as fast as cheetahs
And they are great at jumping over branches.
Need to eat bamboo.
Danger is hunting them.
And they are running for their lives.

Amelia Abdulkadir

Pandas

Panda is like a fluffy cloud
Allowed to cuddle
Needy pandas are starving to eat.
Dreamy pandas, lazy looking,
Amazing beast
Sneaky humans looking for bamboo, but we don't need it as
much as pandas.

Lina Fathalla

The Wind

The wind is howling for it's prey.
The wind is a wolf.
The wind is like a monster.
The rain pours like the ocean.
The cloud is white as the snow.
The wind is a vicious beast.
The storm destroys people's houses.
The lightening is frightening

Lamees Jaroudi

Koala Disaster

Find the reason,
Find the power,
What's the answer to koalas disaster?
This journey has been a rollercoaster ,
Help them out by making a poster.

You might be fearful of this animal,
But then you're a scaredy cat and delusional.

Koala deserves a home ,
Without rent if they die,
I will cry.

Find the reason,
Find the power
What's the answer to koala disaster?

This journey has been a rollercoaster,
Help them out by making a poster.

How would you feel if you were being made extinct
Like a star in the sky
stuck in air
No way out and no way back.

What's the answer to koala disaster?

Aisha Ali

126

Trees

Tall twiggy trees
Provide shade for fresh and blossoming flowers.
Home to many animals
They provide paper power.

Change climate change
Need to recycle paper more
Cutting down too many trees
We should reuse it all the more.

How many trees have got cut down by us
We should not be proud of that
Stop cutting down trees so we can breathe
Stop cutting down trees so we don't leave.

Isa Salaria

Wildlife

Water flows left and right,
Iceberg melting,
Lake full of water,
Decrease of animals,
Land is burning,
Imperative to protect
Forest is green and adventurous
Earth is populating.

Ryan Ali Hamad

Javan Rhinoceros

Javan Rhinos are used for their horn,
If people carry on this may lead to extinction,
Poachers and collectors,
Due to habitat loss Javan Rhinos hide in water,
They live in Indonesia and are found in tropical rainforest,
They are herbivores and they eat leaves, shoots and twigs,
Javan Rhinos live up to 30-45 years in wildlife,
They weigh up to 2.3 tonnes,
Javan Rhinos are the second largest animals after the Asian elephant,
Only 76 of them left,
And stony, grey skin,
Which makes them terrifying and sinister,
Javan Rhinos are the most endangered animal in the world.

Skandar El-Issa

Hunters

Roaming in the mountains
Endangered species
Disappearing from planet

Poachers hunt them
Abducted by human
Nature lover
Danger approaching
Able to run faster

Sideali Hasan

The Endangered Lemurs

People think they're monsters
But they just want to live
Their brains are on a roller coaster
They don't know what's going on
They need help
We could start with a poster
The sound of danger used to be a tiger
But now it's metal clanging
10,000 of them died a year
Their eyes are now filed with fear
Only 2,000 of them are left
They could all die in 3 months
Unless we make a change
They've trained their senses
But people are the monsters
They don't know what they're doing

Sonny Boast

The Snow Leopard

Speedy spotty big cat
Never scared of anyone
Over the mountain ranges
Wild animals that I am

Long tail like a blanket
Ever roaming for food
Our fur, warm and snug,
Powerful legs for jumping,
Asia is where I live
Really bright blue eyes
Delicious blue sheep for me

Leela Allright

White Tigers

Winter I my favourite season.
Happy full clubs after eating a big meal.
I love white tigers with their fluffy white coat of fur.
Tigers fur blending in with the snow.
Eggs of a mother bird sitting next to a pond, ready to eat.

Tigers making a freezing trail across the ice,
Ice melting on a frozen lake.
Gently the white tiger licks the cubs clean.
Environment filled with colourful plants and amazing animals.
Really white tigers are beautiful, so don't kill them. Save them

Katie Lloyd

Tip Toe Away

The water splashes,
The wood creaks,
The animals chatter.
In a blink
The red panda
Smells smoke.

The trees fall;
Clutter, clutter, clutter!
The poachers are here.
Tip-toe away.
No sudden movement or
They'll chop your head
Away
And use your fluff
As some cloth.
So tip-toe away
And no sudden movement.

The slightest of moves
Can attract them.
Don't ask questions
You'll only ask more
Raise your hands and
Come with me.
It's a journey to
Save them with me!

Emily Navickaite Mema

Primrose
Year Six

There's a...

There's a monkey in my living room

There's a monkey in my living room.
And I don't know what to do.
She's tearing up my pillows.

There's a monkey in my living room,
because humans have cut down all the trees.
And now there are no more bananas left.

There's a monkey in my living room.
And now I know what to do.
I'm going to make a poster explaining how people keep
Cutting down the trees.
Will you help me too?

Amelia Ward

There's a jaguar in my kitchen

There's a jaguar in my kitchen and I don't know what to do.
He's breaking all the cabinets and now he's eating all my food.
There's a human in my forest.
They have big machines that destroy all the trees.
They took my siblings and my mum and I'm scared they will take me too.
There's a jaguar in my kitchen.
And now I know why.
I will tell his heart warming story far and wide.
Will you help too?

Jeriah La Touche

There's a leopard in my house

There's a leopard in my house and I don't know what to do.
It's ruining my furniture and it's ruining the walls too.
It's jumping up and down and running round and round.
It's nibbling on my posters and papers.

There's a baby leopard in my house and it needs to leave.
"Oh leopard, why have you come to my house?"
"Humans came to my environment and killed all my family members.
They killed all my friends.
Now I have no one and that's why I came here."

"Oh leopard now I know.
I will fight for you and find you some friends.
I will tell the world.
I will make the world fight for you."

Abdulkhadir Mohamed

134

There's a snow leopard in my front room.

There's a snow leopard in my front room, what should I do?
He's out of control smashing my vase. He's chewed my shoe!
He's eaten my goldfish, and scratched my baby dog.
He jumped all over the place, and got me fired from my job.

I thought that's enough. I shouted at him and said, "Get out."
Then I said, "But one thing, why are you here now?"

He said, "There's humans in my forest killing my family, just for fur.
There are humans in my forest. They killed my father and I don't know
what to do.
So I ran away, far away. I was scared they would kill me too.
I came to you, because I thought I would be ok with you."

"Oh snow leopard, now I know what to do. I will make the biggest
poster.
I will help you save your family and now I want you to stay so we can get
closer.

Alia Rafiq

There's a lion cub in my room

There's a lion cub in my room and I don't know what to do.
He is scratching all my posters and ripping my books too.
He's running around the room and he's just gobbled up my cake.
I was very upset, since it was hard to bake.

There's a lion cub in my room and I don't think it should stay.
So I told the lion cub to take his stuff and go away.
The lion cub looked scared and sad, as he walked towards me.
I wondered if there was something more scary?

"There's a human in my home and I don't know what to do.
They took away my mother and they are coming for me too.
I ran away from my friends. I'm missing them every day.
But I don't think I am welcome so I will not stay."

"Oh lion cub in my room, now I know what to do.
I'll make signs and posters so other people can fight too.
I will keep you safe from the danger in the world outside.
Now that you are with me, I will keep you by my side."

Amira Fahal

There's a turtle in my pool

There's a turtle in my pool and I don't know what to do.
It's splashing all about and it's eating all my food.

Turtle may I ask you, "Why are you here in the first place?"

"My home's all destroyed and it's trashed all day so that's the case.
They throw their waste in my home so I have nowhere to stay.
I don't have a family so I can not go away".

"Don't worry, you can stay. I will protect you all day.
I will spread your story far and wide so you will have your say.
I'm going to help you stop pollution. We will fight together.
We will make posters that shine, help the turtles and change the
weather."

Andra Borzos

There's a gorilla in my bedroom

There's a gorilla in my bedroom and I don't know what to do.
He hates all my food and dislikes my shampoos.
He throws away my plants and fur pillows too!
He destroys all my photos, scratching up my shoes.
I told the disruptive gorilla that he could not stay and he needs to go
away.

"Oh but gorilla before you go, why are you here? I just want to know."

"They're humans in my jungles and I don't know what to do.
They put chemicals in my waters and creating all types of flu.
They're humans in my home and I don't know what to do.
They're burning all my trees, plants and flowers too."

"You poor gorilla now I see. I'll spread your word, until the humans flee.
Your heartfelt story will be around the globe.

Oh I know, I know, people will listen and protest!
From posters to stickers, to books, social media and the news.
I swear to the moon and back I'll show you, the home you know."

Aniyah Prempeh

138

There is a snow leopard in the park

There is a snow leopard in the park and I don't know why he's in the trees.
He's pouncing around and trying to eat the birds from their head to feet.
He is destroying the swings and now he's looking at me like I'm tasty meat.
I feel scared so he needs to leave me alone.
"But before you go, why are you here? I want to know."

"There are humans in my mountain and I don't know why.
They took my parents, which is making me cry.
They are stealing my homelands and I don't know why.
They are burning my grandad's snow forest, almost killing him with such strife.

They are fighting my people and I don't know why.
They are using our land to build houses and factories, every second they strike.

There are humans in my mountain and I don't know why.
They are are making my home too hot so I thought I'd live here and stay with you."

"Oh snow leopard, I know what to do.

I will make a poster to stop you feeling blue.
I swear to god, other people will fight with us too.
Then people will understand but for now, I will be with you."

Anwar Jaabak

There's a rhinoceros in my garden

There's a rhinoceros in my garden and I don't know what to say.
He's trampling on my grass and I so wish he'd go away.
He is chewing on all the trees and flattening all my flowers.
He's stomping on the garden shed. I think it has been hours.
There's a rhinoceros in my garden and he's doing a big poo.
It's been longer than a day now and I still don't know what to do.
Oh rhinoceros in my garden, why will you never go?
There are many trees and plants out there, did you not know?

There are humans in my homeland and I don't know what to do.
They are cutting down all our trees and cutting our horns off too.
We have never done humans any harm but all of these men are armed.
There are humans in my homeland. They've been there for weeks.
Smashing all the flowers and disturbing all the bees.

There are humans in my homeland. They took my family away.
They are digging up the grass. Now you see why I have to stay?

Oh rhinoceros in my garden, I think I have a solution.
I'll make a sign and make it shine. We'll start a revolution!
Maybe then and only then will you have your say.

Oh rhinoceros in my garden, now I really want you to stay.

Bethany Yeates

There's a turtle in my bath

There's a turtle in my bath and I don't know what to do.
She keeps turning on the tap and using my shampoo.
She's a very naughty turtle and she keeps me up all night.
When my mum wakes up to check, she always gets a fright.

So I told the cheeky turtle that she had to go.
Oh turtle in my bath, why are you here? I really want to know.

There are humans in our waters, destroying our homes. I don't know
what to do.
They took my friends and family and I'm scared they'll take me too.
There are humans in our waters, trapping us in nets.
There are humans in our waters and I don't know what to do.
We have done nothing wrong.
I'm so scared so I thought I'd stay with you.

Oh turtle in my bath, now I do know what to do.
I'll fight for your home and stop you feeling blue.
I'll make a poster and it will SHINE. Everyone will see it.
I'll tell all my friends to help you and your family too.
Since you're with me, I'll love and take care of you.

Frankie Williams

There's a jaguar in my bedroom

There's a jaguar in my bedroom roaring.
I don't know why but he's crying.
He's leaping on my table and breaking it.
He's tearing my favourite cushion, bit by bit.

I asked the jaguar to go and leave.
But he came to me and told me his story.
"There's machines in my forest taking palm oil.
They stole my forest and dug the soil.

They took my family away from me.
I had to leave; I was forced to flee.
I didn't know where to evacuate,
So I thought I'd stay with you, where there's no
hate."

"Oh jaguar now I do know what to do.
We will search for a new home, just for you.
We will put a stop to this disaster,
This change of ours will occur faster.

Hassan Babar

There's a polar bear in my garden

There's a polar bear in my garden. What should I do?
He wants to eat all my plants and he screams, "Go!"
Why would he ruin all my flowers, can't he see?
He was hunting but couldn't find anything but a bee.

"Hey polar bear speaking of you, why are you here?"

"I am here, because my family is drowning.
Why aren't people actually caring?"

"You know what, I will make a poster to fight for your rights.
We can save power by turning of the shiny lights.
You will never leave me and everywhere I go, you will be there too."

Isabella Preen

Earth in Peril

World is in danger
But also there is only one ice layer
Can we stop making humans like a slayer
What is more important than nature?

A world needs some supporters
But we only have destroyers
Can we make Earth a better place?
We are just making it into a disgrace.

As we cough from the dirty skies
Be careful it is full of lies
Can we help our land?
But instead stop it to expand.

As the world has gone sad in emotions
We made it even more distraught in pollution
Can we see the world has turned bad?
The cause has made animals mad

Reza Mousavi Khalkhali

144

There is a panda in my garden

There is a panda in my garden and I don't know what to do.
She is tearing up my books and throwing my food.
There is a panda in my garden and I don't know what to do.
She is chewing on my grass thinking it's bamboo.
So I told the dreadful panda to go away.
"But panda before you go, why are you in my garden? I really want to know".
"There are humans in my forest and I don't know what to do.
There are humans in my forest, and they're cutting down my trees too."
"Now I know, oh dear, panda now I know.
I will help put a stop to this terrible disaster.
I will put up posters and I will ask people to help you too."

Maria Ahmad

There's a panda in my garden

There's a panda in my garden and he is driving me cuckoo.
He takes all my fruit and likes my bamboo.
I told the naughty panda that he has to go away and he frowns without a say.
Just before you leave, I really want to know why you came to stay.
There's a metal monster in my forest cutting down the trees.
No matter how I plead he chops the trees with ease.
It took my parents from me. Now you want me to leave.
Panda, I know now why you came to stay: you wanted to be safe from the monster's blaze!
So we shall protect your home from the monster's gaze

Ruby Ike-Michael

145

There's a monkey in my home

There's a monkey in my home.
And I don't know what to do.
He took my book and my shampoo.
There's a monkey in my home,
because humans have taken his family.
And he doesn't know what to do.
There's a monkey in my home.
And now I know what to do.
I'm going to tell people.
Will you help me too?

Sabrina Mamadjonova

There's an Amur Leopard in my garden

There's a leopard in my garden and I don't know what to do.
He is jumping around, as if he's a crazy kangaroo.
He is shouting and knocking down all my shampoo.
The leopard is gulping down all my expensive shoes.
There's a leopard in my garden and I want to know why.

"The humans have invaded my home and I really want to cry.
They killed all my family and I didn't say goodbye."

There's a leopard in my garden and now I'm not confused.
I'm going to spread the word that you're getting abused.
I will help you. Don't worry you have nothing to loose.
You can live and stay in my garden for as long as you choose.

Sara Shahid

146

There's a jaguar in my kitchen

There's a jaguar in my kitchen eating all of my shoes.
He is jumping around my kitchen and eating all of my food.
He is growling at my jaguar coloured shampoo.

There's a jaguar in my kitchen and I don't know what to do.
There's a jaguar in my kitchen and I want him to go away.
So I told the naughty jaguar that he couldn't stay.
"Before you go naughty jaguar, did you come here for my hay
Or did you come here because you are not okay?
Why did you come to my kitchen? I really do want to know."

"There are humans in my forest and I do not know where to go.
They are chopping down my trees and taking away my home.
They are trying to take my skin off my bones.
So now you know why I came here and escaped that crime."

"Now I know what to do, I will make a sign.
Everybody will know your story and know why you can't climb.
Now jaguar you can stay in my kitchen, you know I don't mind."

Scarlett Hamilton

There's a snow leopard in my bedroom

There's a snow leopard in my room and I don't know what to do.
There's a snow leopard in my room and she keeps borrowing my shoes.

She's eating up my poor goldfish and can't stop chewing my teddies.
She's scratching all my posters and tearing up my books.
She's smashing all my windows and growling at my cat.
She's broken everything I own. She really needs to go.

Why are you in my bedroom? I really want to know.

"There are humans in my homeland and I don't know what to do.
They took away my family and I'm afraid they will take me too.
They destroyed my land and scared away my prey.
There are humans in my home. Now you see why I want to stay with you."

"Oh snow leopard now I know what to do.

I will spread your story far in the world.
I know there are kind people in the world.
I will make sure you are home safely."

Serene Pelham

There's a panda in my garden

There's a panda in my garden eating bamboo.
I'm really confused and I don't know what to do.
He's climbing all my plants and throwing them away.
Panda, you should go now or are you here to stay?

"I'm here as humans are taking my home away.
This is the whole reason I was here to play.
They are cutting down trees for your palm oil.
We need many more trees to plant in the soil."

Oh panda, I know these times can be really tough.
I know that humans can be very careless and rough.
I promise that I will help you forever be.
You can come to me, when you need me.

Thalita Corrazzin

The Death of the Earth

We are destroying the nature
The tree works so hard to clean the air
They need to help the Earth to be fair
The Earth is dying in our hands
The animals are in fear of us
We need to stop the madness

Sufyan Hussain

There's a tiger in my school

There's a tiger in my school.
He always swims in the pool.
When he plays, he is rough.
He likes to break stuff.
He eats everything.
And he breaks the swings.
He takes long to eat.
He has big feet.
He is not that funny.
He acts like a bunny.
He likes everyone's shoes.
I don't know what to do.

I asked him, "Why are you here?
Shouldn't you be there?
At your habitat."

"Everyone says that.
I'm here, because of humans.
Just like pumas."

"I know what I'm going to do.
I'll spread this message just for you.
I am very sorry.
Please don't worry.

Can you please stay.
Don't go away."

Uzair Patawala

150

There's an Amur Leopard in my Room

There's an Amur leopard in my room and it's getting on my nerves.
She's breaking all my picture frames and gobbling up the birds.
She's turned my room into a dump and now it looks absurd.
She's jumping on my pristine bed and doing smelly turds.
I wish that she would go away and let me hear my thoughts.
There's no such thing as peace and quiet, as all I hear is, "ROOOAR!"
She's broken everything I own; I really want to cry.
But please can I just ask you; you are in my bedroom - why?

There are humans in my forest and I had to run away.
They've taken everything I own and made it hard to stay.
There are humans in my forest and I had to run away.
There's no more food, so I am hungry every single day.
There are humans in my forest and there's nowhere else to hide.
You asked me why I'm here with you and now I've told you why.

Oh, Amur leopard in my room, now I have a good idea!
You may not have a home, but for now you'll be safe here.
I'll tell everyone that I know about the terrors you've faced.
And then your trees will grow and thrive - you'll go back to that place!
Oh, Amur leopard in my room, I will make people see.
They'll see you have a life back there - we'll fight till you run free.

Zara Fuzesi

What is Happening to Nature?

The nature is clean. We are making it not clean
We're eating the plants
Killing the bulls
We're catching the trees and killing the trees
We're annoying the animals
Killing the snakes making them belts
We killing the elephant by buying his teeth
The animals are dying
We have to stop killing them
The animals are dying because
We are killing them
We have trees and we're cutting thousands of trees
Killing the bears and making the jackets

Abubokar Hasan

We Should Fix Up

We are destroying the life of animals and nature
We are making danger
We are not helping the animals
We are demolishing all of the all of the land and nature

They cut down trees
We are taking the leaves
We should stop pollution
We eat all the animals with our teeth

We don't have a magic to fix the ocean
That is why we should join the animal helper group
We should speak up for all of the damage
Humans should not eat animals like we eat soup

Yusuf Ahmed

There is a Gorilla in My Room

There is a gorilla in my room,
and I don't know what to do.
He ate my rice and stole my shampoo
and now I don't know what to do.

There is a gorilla in my room,
because humans have cut down the trees in his forest.
As well as destroying all his food.

There is a gorilla in my room
and I finally know what to do.
I'm going to tell everyone the truth.
Will you help me too?

Sara Al-Kooh

Highbury
Year Six

Our World

Gorilla

Gorillas are animals we must protect.
Because unfortunately, they're under threat.
Would you seriously want to kill an innocent primate?
When all they want to do is play in their hot climate.
Although for now they're full of laughter,
There won't be any left soon after.
Poachers think killing makes them strong,
Little do they know it's very wrong.
Each gorilla dies,it's their fate.
But who will be the one to mate?
At night, the poachers like to fight.
Since they're out of the gorillas' sight.
Why can't they live happy and fair?
Instead,each day they die by snares!
When gorillas see a human stranger
They don't know that they're in danger.
While they humans cut down the trees,
The gorillas get scared and try to flee.
The poachers load up their guns.
Do people really think that's fun?
Maybe they should leave them be.
All the gorillas would like to be free.
The father will eventually die.
Now the gorillas must say goodbye.

Audrey Sofiyan

Gorilla

Happy and harmless
Gorillas live
Each day
Then here come the poachers to
Steal their toys away
Setting snare
to entrap and kill
The gorillas are crying as
they lay dying.

Ayah Latouché

Gorilla

In mountains the baby gorilla play
In the mountains where they should stay
In the jungle the baby gorillas stay
While the mother gorilla gets taken away
In rainforest the baby gorilla are happy
While the mother gorilla is unhappy
In the wild the baby gorillas roam
While the mother gorilla protect the home

Baahir Omari

Gorillas Dying

Gorillas are dying
And they're crying

In the night the gorillas rest
A time the poachers love best

Up in the mountains the gorillas play
But the poachers are coming their way

The gorillas are smart
But they have emotions that break their heart

The unique gorilla are strong
But against a poacher they are weak

Darioush Mirani

Gorilla

The gorillas howl unaware of the dangers in the dark
The smart poachers
Gorillas get caught
Baby gorillas are upset and the poachers are pests.
Gorillas are scared
Of the demons

Dave Casalme

The Gorilla Poem

Living in fear because of the snare
The gorillas are strong but they haven't done anything wrong
Why are there poachers? This is all torture
The poachers are in sight but the gorillas are the light
The poachers think they will get their prey but the gorillas say not
today

Donia Boudal Moumni

The Destroyed Earth

Our planet is being destroyed,
Trees and animals are dying.
And now humans are upset,
While sighing and crying.

Plants are dead and trees have been cut,
There is no more beautiful land.
The sea will no longer have
Any seaweed and plastic is on the sand.

Animals are becoming trapped,
And have been continuously expiring.
So, many people are panicking,
While their pets are perishing and humans are crying.

We humans should stop burning fossil fuels
And also put an end to polluting.
Workers should not cut down trees,
instead go to a protest and start saluting.

Hanna Ashraf

Gorilla

The gorillas bark,
Unaware of the dangers in the dark,
They are smart,
But something breaks their heart.
It's a hill,
Full of kill.
One by one they get shot,
It's a plot.
Near the swamps,
It's full of gorillas,
Captured by the killers,
Ready to be transported to Europe.

Leon Fumagalli

Gorillas

Gorillas live in fear
But the poachers don't care

Gorillas have feelings
Stripped away like bananas peelings

But while the healthy Gorillas eat
Against the poachers they are weak

Raymond Wintz

Dying Gorillas

Gorillas are killed
Against their will
Soon the bangs will seize
Like a troop of a disease
Soon the silverbacks will retire
Because the poachers will fire
Poachers are in hiding
Soon the gorillas will be flying
Soon when gorillas come out and play
Not knowing what will come their way
Then soon their dad
Will take his final breath
Then soon poachers will cause
His death
Those innocent gorillas
Swaying and playing
Unaware of the snares
That are unfair.

Lily Leng

Gorillas

As gorillas roam
Through their mountatin home
You come with guns and set your snares
How dare you hunt gorillas, do you think that's fair?
When it is night you poachers hunt best
When you find the gorilla troop
You commit the biggest sins
When you kill the gorilla group

Tamera Barlow Prehay

Gorilla

Why do we hurt these innocent creatures?
In the mountains they are an important features
A large African ape
Has no chance to escape
Every time innocent baby gorillas are having fun
The danger has already begun
They are never going to recover
We do this forever
Gorillas are being killed
Against their wills
They all cry
As we lie
We torture them as much as we can
While we take all their land

Listen to these wise words
As it can save lives

Drew MacDonald

162

Gorilla

In the mountains beautiful baby gorillas play
Unaware of the danger planning to come their way
Gorillas sleeping or playing and laying
The danger came screaming and yelling
The gorillas are never to be found

Fatma Kheleef

Gorilla

It is not fair for these silverbacks
They are constantly being tracked
These shy animals are under threat
It is never correct
Baby gorillas playing with their mates
They do not know about their fate
Poachers lay these dangerous snares
They should know that it is very unfair
Getting their loaded up guns
They think that killing these apes is fun
Just because you will look strong
It still means that poaching is wrong
As these primates depart
Think about their family's heart

Anisa Hassan

Gorilla

You are just gentle giants
Though beware of the tyrants
While the troop cries in despair
The humans laugh without a care
Poachers walk on a cracking stick
The gorillas time continues to tick
The poachers will come out at night
When the gorillas have no sight
The poacher points his gun
The mother says goodbye to the sun
Then her world turns black...

Jasmine Dzugaj

Gorilla

In the rainforest, where baby gorillas play
The mother gorilla says to stay away from the danger far away
The silverback is worried for his troop
The poachers are planning to kill the group
Danger comes and gorillas run through mud
So when the poachers find the gorillas there will be blood
Poachers walk near the gorillas like a ghost
Away goes the gorilla who the mother loves the most

Verona Volta

Gorilla

Up in the clouds baby gorillas play
Up in the mountains to stay their way
Gorillas are kind not to be found
If you're making a silly sound
At night gorillas sleeping
Poachers will come that is sleeping
Poachers are mean
Not to be seen
Be smart
Have a heart
Run away
And you can stay away

Luna Berhane

Gorillas

Gorillas are strong
But they haven't done anything wrong

You poachers torture gorillas with snare
This could never be fair

Why should they live in fear
Why should you go near?

Mya Chevannes

Gorilla

We must protect
They are under threat
When they aren't even killers
We must protect gorillas
As they are pillars

Gorillas are harmful
But they stare in despair
And we just don't care

Farewell
Animals are getting tortured
This large African ape

The largest - they try to escape
We have to try to be fair
With what they bear
With the pain they share
With human being like us

Farewell.

We will never be fair with
Guns everywhere

Hend Ali

Danger and Destruction

What are we doing to nature?
Instead of letting them grow
We are destroying and hurting it
Rather than digging and cutting and pulling them up,
We need to start to sow.

Our environment is in danger,
We need to let our nature breathe,
Get rid of the pollution,
Or they are going to leave.

The poor plants are dying
We need to treasure and save our plants
Too much pollution
Will make them go slant

Anaya Sheikh

The Plastic Earth

The water is full of plastic
The Earth is full of dirt
The trees are falling like dominoes
Humans are now hurt

Our Nature can't survive
People are now crying
The sea is full of plastic
And trees are dying

Animals are running like a race car
The chicken sadly are killed
Animals are very upset
Our bellies will no longer be filled

What do we do?

Humans should treat the trees fairly
They be stopping the forest fires
They should stop, learn about the nature
Or they will be known as bare faced liars

Hafsa Mohammed

168

Damaged Earth

Our world is damaged.
We humans are destroying our home.
We need to stop and help
Save the animals.
Remember the Earth will always be on loan

Our environment is hurt.
Fossil fuels are burning,
We humans are polluting and
We need to start learning.

These poor animals are being murdered.
We need to stop eating meat.
We humans need to take care
And start eating wheat.

We are destroying land.
Animals are dying
Because we humans are greedy
While children are crying.

Zaina Ragab

Thank you

Thank you so much for reading this book.

The children of Anson Primary School care about our planet, the animals which inhabit it and the impact of our actions.

They ask you and future generations to support projects which go some way to making our world a better place to live.